my first book of questions and answers

trucks and diggers

James Pickering

p

This is a Parragon Book
First published in 2002

Parragon
Queen Street House
4 Queen Street
Bath BA1 1HE, UK

Produced by

David West ⚐ Children's Books
7 Princeton Court
55 Felsham Road
Putney
London SW15 1AZ

British Library Cataloguing-in-Publication Data

A catalogue record for this book is available from
the British Library.

ISBN 0-75258-459-6

Printed in China

Designers
Axis Design, Aarti Parmar, Rob Shone,
Fiona Thorne

Illustrator
Dud Moseley (SGA)

Cartoonist
Peter Wilks (SGA)

Editor
Ross McLaughness

CONTENTS

4 Were there trucks before engines?

5 Which coach ran on steam?

5 What did steam trucks look like?

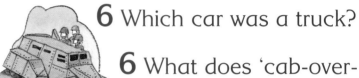

6 Which car was a truck?

6 What does 'cab-over-engine' mean?

7 What replaced steam trucks?

8 Which trucks bend in the middle?

8 Which trucks have piggybacks?

9 Which trucks deliver cars?

10 What is a low-loader?

11 Which trucks can travel through water?

11 What are caterpillar tracks?

12 How do trucks stop?

12 What is a jack-knife?

13 Why do trucks have so many gears?

14 What is a customised truck?

14 What are tractor tuggers?

15 Which trucks crush cars?

16 What is a road train?

16 Which is the biggest truck?

17 What is a digger?

18 Where do truckers sleep?

18 Where do truckers eat?

19 How do truckers talk to each other?

20 Which small trucks carry heavy loads?

20 Which trucks carry logs?

21 Do trucks pull aeroplanes?

22 Which trucks are freezing?

22 How is petrol delivered?

23 What is a container truck?

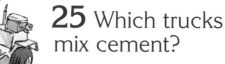

24 Which truck eats rubbish?

25 What is a wrecker?

25 Which trucks mix cement?

26 Which trucks are hospitals?

26 Which truck puts out fires?

27 Which trucks are safe?

28 Which trucks travel through the desert?

28 Are there truck races?

29 Can you race a pickup?

30 What is a bulldozer?

30 Which digger does lots of jobs?

31 What is a mobile crane?

32 Index

Dray-horses and cart

Steam truck

? Were there trucks before engines?

Before engines were invented, heavy loads were pulled on carts by teams of large dray-horses. Strong dray-horses were also used to pull ploughs on farms before motorised tractors were invented.

Which coach ran on steam?

Dr Church's steam coach was built in England in 1833. Up to 50 passengers rode on it, on long journeys between cities. It must have been very noisy and uncomfortable.

Dr Church's steam coach

What did steam trucks look like?

Steam trucks looked like steam trains, with large engines, big iron wheels and smoky funnels. They were so big and heavy that they ruined the roads.

TRUE OR FALSE?

Early trucks were huge.

FALSE. Steam trucks were the largest vehicles on the road, but they were still much smaller than modern trucks.

Steam trucks were very slow.

TRUE. In England, someone had to walk in front of the first trucks, with a red flag to warn other road-users.

Model 'T' Ford truck

? Which car was a truck?

Many early trucks were really cars which had been given extra parts and made stronger, to carry heavy loads. This 1919 truck was based on the popular Model 'T' Ford car.

? What does 'cab-over-engine' mean?

A cab-over-engine truck is a truck where the driver's cab is on top of the engine. When the engine needs to be repaired, the whole cab tips forward to give the mechanic a good look.

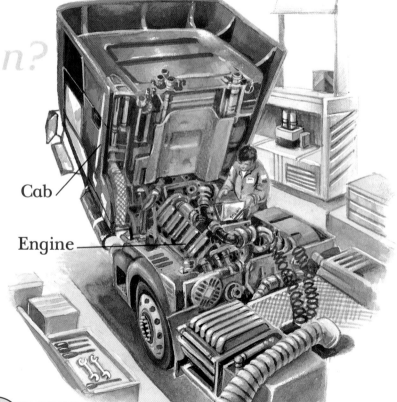

Cab

Engine

What replaced steam trucks?

Steam trucks were noisy, dirty and not very reliable. Petrol-powered trucks first appeared in 1896, and were much more popular. These days, most trucks run on diesel fuel.

Dennis

7

TRUE OR FALSE?

Some trucks had no tyres.

TRUE. Before air-filled tyres were invented, trucks had huge, heavy wheels made of metal.

Anyone can drive a truck.

FALSE. It's more difficult to drive a truck than an ordinary car. Truck drivers have to pass a test before they're allowed to drive a truck on the road.

Which trucks bend in the middle?

Long articulated trucks, which pull separate trailers, bend in the middle – if they didn't, they wouldn't be able to turn round sharp corners. Shorter trucks, which are built in one piece and don't bend in the middle, are called rigid trucks.

Articulated truck

Which trucks have piggybacks?

New trucks are sometimes delivered by being towed behind another truck, like a trailer. This means that there's less wear on the new trucks' tyres, less fuel is burned and only one driver is needed to move several trucks.

? *Which trucks deliver cars?*

? Transporters can deliver up to ten cars at a time. The cars are driven on to the transporter up ramps, and they're very carefully strapped down during the journey, so they don't roll off!

Transporter

Piggyback trucks

Trucks sneeze.

TRUE. Have you ever noticed how trucks make a hissing noise, like a sneeze? That's the sound of air escaping from their brakes.

Truckers set their trucks on fire.

FALSE. But drivers in very cold countries do make fires under their trucks, to stop the diesel fuel from freezing.

Low-loader

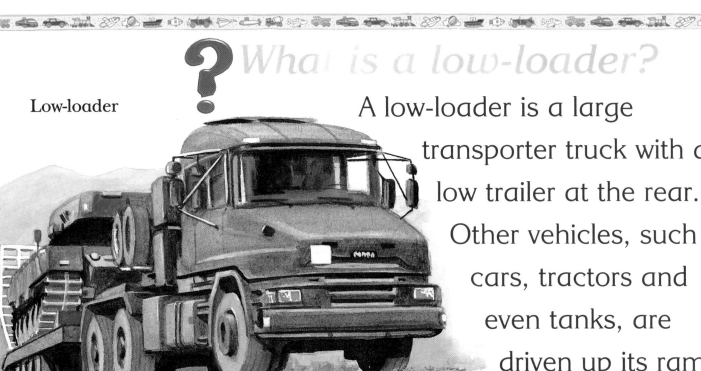

A low-loader is a large transporter truck with a low trailer at the rear. Other vehicles, such as cars, tractors and even tanks, are driven up its ramps and on to the trailer.

Half-track army truck

Caterpillar track

Which trucks can travel through water?

Special army trucks, called amphibious trucks, can travel on land and through shallow rivers. The underside of the truck is tightly sealed so that water can't flood into the cab or into the engine.

Amphibious truck

What are caterpillar tracks?

Caterpillar tracks are knobbly strips of metal or rubber, which wrap around the wheels of tanks, bulldozers and other off-road vehicles. They stop the wheels from getting stuck in muddy or sandy ground.

Some trucks wear armour.

TRUE. Some army trucks are covered in very strong metal armour plating to protect them.

Tanks had caterpillar tracks first.

FALSE. Caterpillar tracks were first used to stop tractors getting stuck in muddy fields. Soldiers guessed they would work just as well on tanks.

Air-lines

How do trucks stop?

Trucks use air-brakes to stop. An air compressor in the truck sucks in air and squashes it. When the driver presses the brake pedal, the squashed air travels along coiled air-lines and pushes brake shoes against the wheels, slowing them down.

What is a jack-knife?

A jack-knife is a dangerous accident where a truck slows down, but its trailer slides sideways out of control, sometimes spilling its load on to the road. A jack-knife is named after a knife with a folding blade.

This transporter has jack-knifed.

? *Why do trucks have so many gears?*

Trucks sometimes have over 15 gears, compared to only five or six in a car. Heavy trucks need plenty of low gears to go up and down steep hills, and higher gears to cruise along the open road.

TRUE OR FALSE?

Trucks aren't able to climb steep hills.

FALSE. Trucks can climb hills, but because they're much heavier than cars, they can't do it very quickly!

Truckers need to rest.

TRUE. Truck drivers have to take regular breaks in case they get sleepy at the wheel and cause an accident.

? What is a customised truck?

? Truckers often want their trucks to look different from everyone else's. They can customise their trucks by painting them with bright patterns and colours, or by adding extra lights or shiny metal bodywork.

Customised truck

Tractor tugger

? What are tractor tuggers?

Tractor tuggers are powered by fiery aircraft engines! They have to pull a load of 100 tonnes (as heavy as 100 family cars) for 100 m in special competitions.

Which trucks crush cars?

? Monster trucks are small pickup trucks, which have been fitted with enormous dumper-truck wheels. They take part in races, and drive over large obstacles, including cars, crushing them as flat as pancakes!

Monster truck

Some trucks can jump.

TRUE. Stunt drivers drive their trucks very quickly up ramps, and fly over rows of cars and other obstacles.

Trucks can do wheelies.

TRUE. By revving the engine very hard, stunt drivers can lift the front wheels of their trucks into the air. That's called doing a wheelie.

? What is a road train?

A road train is a very strong truck, which pulls not one, but several long trailers. Road trains make very long journeys in big countries, such as Australia.

Road train

? Which is the biggest truck?

The biggest truck in the world is a dumper truck called the Terex Titan. Each of its wheels is twice as high as a person, and weighs as much as three family cars!

Terex Titan

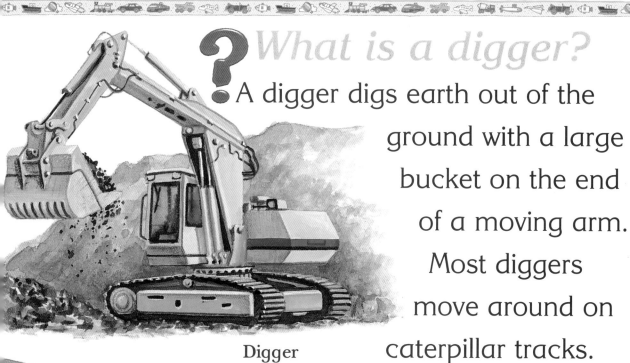

?*What is a digger?*

?A digger digs earth out of the ground with a large bucket on the end of a moving arm. Most diggers move around on caterpillar tracks.

Digger

Terex Titan travels on the road.

FALSE. Terex Titan is too big to travel on the road. Instead it's taken to pieces, and each part is carried on a transporter.

Some trucks need help from the police.

TRUE. Trucks pulling very large loads need the police to travel with them, to warn other drivers to get out of the way.

Where do truckers sleep?

Truckers are often on the road for several days at a time, and need somewhere to sleep away from home. Some truckers sleep in their cabs, in a bed behind the seats.

Where do truckers eat?

There are truck stops on main roads all over the world, where truckers can get a bite to eat, fill up with fuel, wash their clothes, and sometimes even have their hair cut!

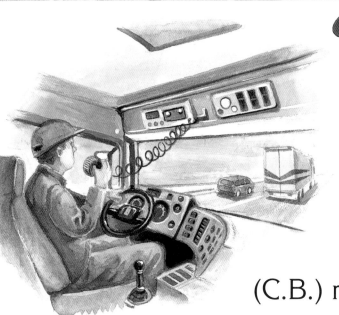

? How do truckers talk to each other?

Truckers talk to each other on the move using citizens' band (C.B.) radio. Every trucker has a nickname, and can warn other drivers of hazards, such as traffic jams or bad weather.

Truck stop

TRUE OR FALSE?

Trucks are scrubbed clean.

TRUE. Most truck stops have a drive-through truck wash, where trucks are scrubbed clean with huge soapy brushes.

Trucks never break down.

FALSE. Trucks do break down sometimes. There are usually teams of mechanics and plenty of spare parts at truck stops.

Forklift trucks

Forklift trucks can carry heavy loads around factories, on wooden platforms called pallets. The driver slides the forks underneath the pallets, lifts them into the air, and moves them to another part of the factory.

Which trucks carry logs?

Loggers are large trucks, which carry logs from forests to factories. Logs are much too heavy to be put on a truck by hand, so a logger has its own crane that picks up the logs and puts them on the back of the truck.

Do trucks pull aeroplanes?

Airport tugs are strong enough to pull large aeroplanes. These short trucks fit under an aeroplane's nose, and fix on to its front wheel.

Airport tug

Logger

Freezer truck

? Which trucks are freezing?

A freezer truck is like a big fridge on wheels. It's used to transport food, such as ice cream, which has to stay cold in case it melts.

? How is petrol delivered?

? Petrol is delivered to petrol stations in tankers. A tanker can carry enough petrol to fill up about 500 family cars. The petrol is pumped into a large tank, buried beneath the station.

Petrol tanker

Container truck

? What is a container truck?

Many of the goods you see in the shops are made overseas, and arrive on ships in metal boxes called containers. The containers are lifted off the ships and put on to large container trucks, which drive them straight to the shops.

TRUE OR FALSE?

Some trucks tip up.

TRUE. A tipper truck has a special lifting body, which tips up, so that its load simply slides out of the back.

You can fly in a truck.

FALSE. But cherry pickers lift people into the air on a long arm, to do jobs such as changing bulbs in street lamps.

Garbage truck

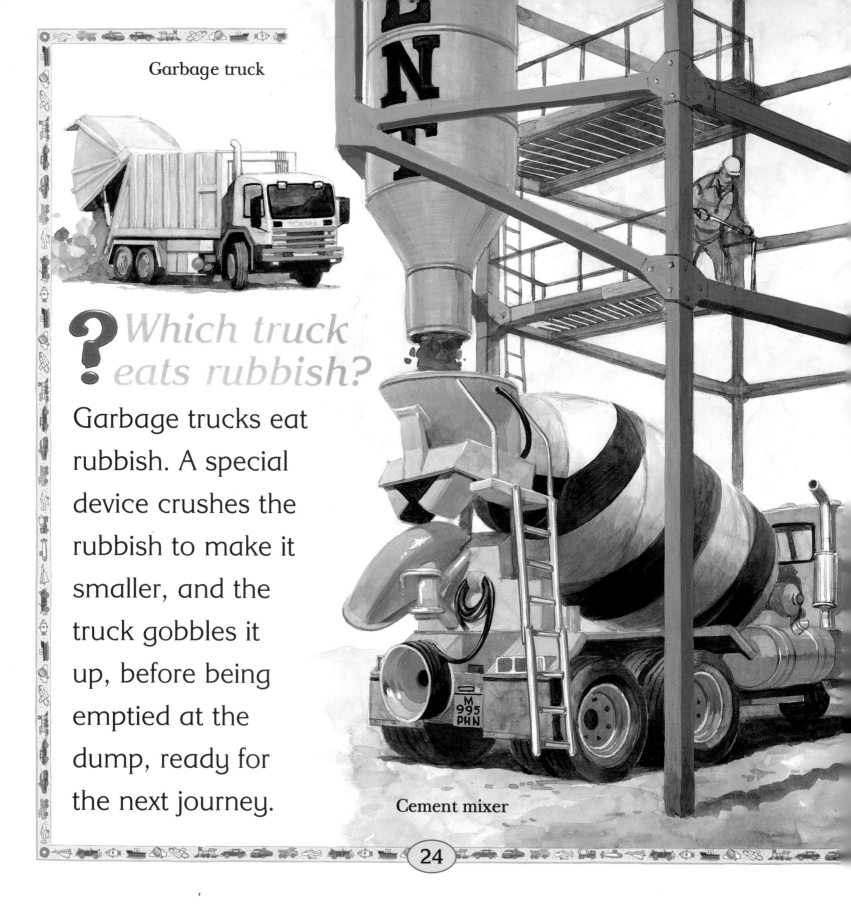

? Which truck eats rubbish?

Garbage trucks eat rubbish. A special device crushes the rubbish to make it smaller, and the truck gobbles it up, before being emptied at the dump, ready for the next journey.

Cement mixer

What is a wrecker?

'Wrecker' is the name for a large North American breakdown truck, which can tow away other trucks or cars, if they've broken down or had an accident.

Wrecker

Which trucks mix cement?

Cement and other ingredients are mixed together in a cement mixer, to make concrete, which is used to make buildings. The ingredients are put in the mixer's drum, which spins around. When the concrete is ready, it's poured out of the cement mixer.

25

TRUE OR FALSE?

Garbage trucks pick up rubbish.

TRUE. Some garbage trucks can pick up dustbins with mechanical arms, shake them until they're empty, then put them down again.

Trucks have to be weighed.

TRUE. When trucks pass from one country or state into another, they often have to be weighed, to work out how much tax they need to pay.

Which trucks are hospitals?

An ambulance is a small truck full of emergency equipment, which takes ill people to hospital quickly. But in areas where there are no hospitals, doctors and nurses treat patients in larger trucks called mobile hospitals, where they can even perform life-saving operations.

Mobile hospital

Which truck puts out fires?

Fire trucks are packed full of equipment to put out fires. They have powerful hoses, medical equipment, axes for breaking down doors, and ladders to reach fires in tall buildings.

Which trucks are safe?

Armour-plated security vans collect money from shops and banks. It's important that the money isn't stolen, so it's kept in a safe, which even the van driver can't open.

Security van

Fire truck

TRUE OR FALSE?

All fire trucks have one driver.

FALSE. Fire trucks with very long ladders, have a second driver who sits on the ladder, steering it safely around corners.

Some fire trucks squirt foam.

TRUE. It's very dangerous to squirt water at fires caused by electricity. Firefighters put out electrical fires with foam instead.

The Paris-Dakar rally is a very long race for cars and motorbikes through the dusty Sahara desert. Back-up trucks come along too, full of spare parts, in case any of the racers crashes or breaks down.

Paris-Dakar back-up truck

? *Are there truck races?*

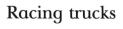

Racing trucks

You can race almost anything on wheels, including trucks. There are bumpy cross-country rallies, and races around tracks. Some racing trucks are even powered by huge jet engines, and can whizz along more quickly than an express train!

Pickup racer

? *Can you race a pickup?*

Pickup trucks are small trucks, which are normally used for carrying small loads, but they can also be raced. Souped-up versions, with low bodies, streamlined shapes and extra-powerful engines race around circuits in America.

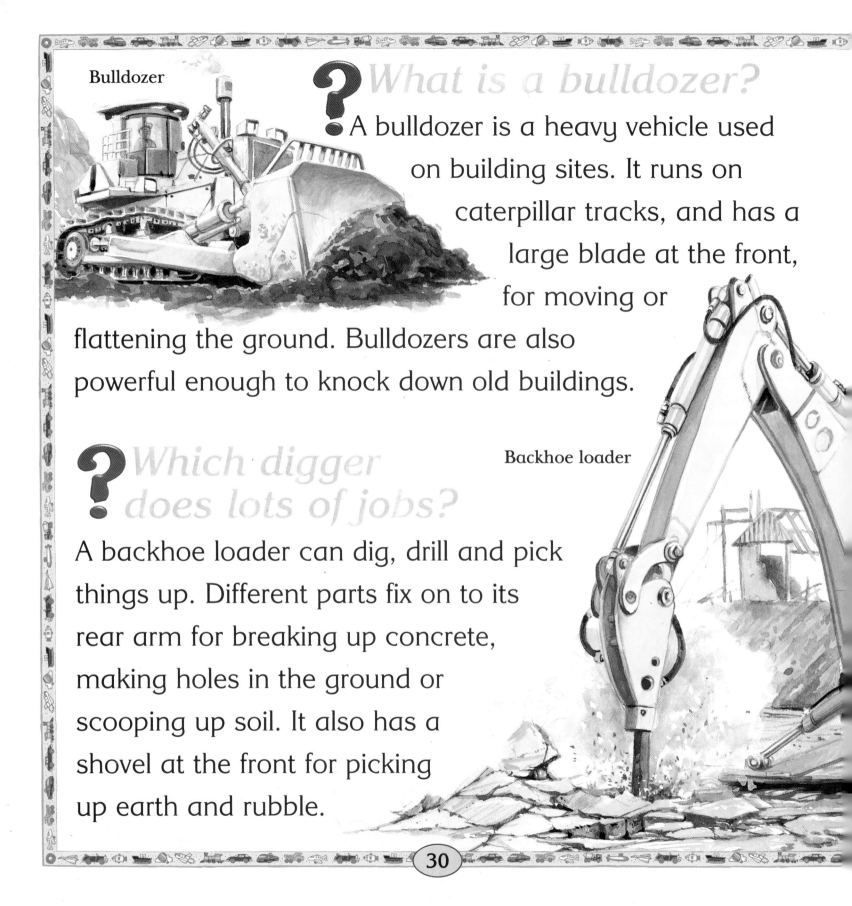

Bulldozer

A bulldozer is a heavy vehicle used on building sites. It runs on caterpillar tracks, and has a large blade at the front, for moving or flattening the ground. Bulldozers are also powerful enough to knock down old buildings.

? Which digger does lots of jobs?

Backhoe loader

A backhoe loader can dig, drill and pick things up. Different parts fix on to its rear arm for breaking up concrete, making holes in the ground or scooping up soil. It also has a shovel at the front for picking up earth and rubble.

? *What is a mobile crane?*

? A mobile crane is part truck and part crane. It can be driven on to building sites, where the driver operates the crane from a cab at the back, lifting heavy loads of concrete or metal.

Mobile crane

Index

airport tugs 21

ambulances 26

amphibious trucks 11

backhoe loaders 30

brakes 12

bulldozers 30

C.B. radio 19

cab-over-engine 6

caterpillar tracks 11, 30

cement mixers 25

container trucks 23

customised trucks 14

diggers 17

Dr Church's steam coach 5

dray-horses 4

fire trucks 26, 27, 29

forklift trucks 20

freezer trucks 22

garbage trucks 24

gears 13

jack-knife 12

loggers 20

low-loader 10

mobile crane 31

mobile hospitals 26

Model T Ford 6

monster trucks 15

Paris-Dakar rally 28

petrol tankers 22

pickup trucks 15, 29

piggyback 8

racing trucks 28, 29

road trains 16

security vans 27

steam trucks 5, 7

Terex Titan 16, 21

tractor tuggers 14

transporter 9

truck stops 18, 19

wreckers 25